CW00400465

House 4 Regent St Cambridge CB2 1BY
e: Cambridge 358977

With compliments

CAMBRIDGE
CITY COUNCIL

Community
Development

Working for the Community

Richard Seager is a housing consultant. He has previously worked for the Commission for Racial Equality, for a housing association and in local government. He was responsible for the first report on racial harassment on local authority housing estates published in 1981 by the CRE.

Joanna Jeffery is a housing consultant. She has previously worked for Department of the Environment and in local government.

ELIMINATING RACIAL HARASSMENT

A guide to housing policies and procedures

Richard Seager and Joanna Jeffery

LEMOS ASSOCIATES
LONDON

Published in Great Britain 1994 by

Lemos Associates
20 Pond Square
London N6 6BA

Telephone 081-348 8263

© Lemos Associates 1994

ISBN 1-898001-01-4

A CIP catalogue record for this book is
available from the British Library

Phototypeset by Kerrypress Ltd, Luton
Printed by BPCC Wheatons, Exeter

CONTENTS

FOREWORD

by Herman Ouseley, Chair of the
Commission for Racial Equality

In its statement of purpose, the Commission for Racial Equality has identified a society free from racial prejudice and attacks as being a key pre-requisite for a just society based on racial equality and free from racial discrimination.

The problem of racial attacks and harassment on the street, in schools, shops and in the home continues to cause growing concern. Attacks in the home, both on the person and on the property, are the most serious because they so fundamentally undermine an individual's sense of security and well-being. If the home cannot be regarded as safe, then nowhere can. The effects of racial attacks divide communities and hurt the victims, their families and friends. Even the perpetrator suffers as everyone is adversely affected.

The CRE has issued its statutory code of practice in rented housing, compliance with which is a requirement on local authorities and housing associations. In this, the need for action on racial attacks and harassment is stressed. In addition local authorities have a duty to tackle racial harassment effectively as part of their duties to promote racial equality under section 71 of the Race Relations Act.

It is essential that all landlords, especially those of social housing, have effective policies and procedures for dealing with racial harassment, but the evidence remains that existing policies and procedures are failing. There is still little reason for confidence that the problem is always being reported, much less solved.

Evidence for this is in the continued massive under-reporting of the problem. The British Crime Survey suggested an annual total of more than 130,000. Only 7,793 were reported to the police in 1992.

Recent years have seen a growing recognition of the reality of racial harassment at or near the home, but problems continue to be found in the way policies aimed at supporting the victims of racial attacks and taking action against perpetrators are not implemented effectively. More needs to be done and the guidance in this book provides an important framework for the development of successful strategies to help to eliminate racial harassment.

INTRODUCTION

Purpose of this guide

In 1991, the then Home Secretary, Kenneth Baker, said in describing a case of racial harassment from West Yorkshire in the Foreword to the Second Report of the Inter-Departmental Racial Attacks Group:

> This case illustrates the challenge and the opportunity for all of us with the responsibility to tackle racial attacks and harassment . . . The challenge is to overcome what is unquestionably the most obnoxious and destructive aspect of the racial discrimination that still festers in our country. The opportunity is to do so in partnership – between Government and agencies, police services and local authorities, community groups and victims. Nothing casts a greater blot on our civilised society than people's lives being ruined because of who they are – black, Asian, white or whatever group. Nothing demands greater commitment, energy and co-ordination in resolving it.

In addition to the strong moral and practical imperatives for action to stop racial harassment, there are
penalties for inaction. Local authority landlords may
face claims of maladministration by their tenants for
failure to take action against racial harassment.

In 1993 Bristol City Council was ordered to pay
£10,000 compensation to a mixed race family who had
suffered racial harassment by neighbours for a period of
11 years. The family complained to the local government ombudsman who found the council guilty of
maladministration. The council had failed to give proper
advice, failed to record and investigate complaints,
failed to liaise effectively with other agencies and failed
to monitor developments in the case.

This guide sets out an overview of what a racial
harassment policy should cover. It gives examples of
good practice in dealing with racial harassment, and
provides some specimen forms for recording incidents
of harassment and action taken.

The emphasis throughout this guide and its companion volumes, details of which are at the back of the
book, is to offer straightforward practical advice to
assist policy makers, staff and managers. Experience
shows that early action is often essential to prevent
incidents of harassment escalating, but staff and managers sometimes hesitate to intervene. This guide,
together with its companion volumes, should provide
staff with the confidence and knowledge to intervene
and prevent escalation.

Those with experience of dealing with incidents of
racial harassment will know that there are often no easy
solutions. The approach taken in this manual does not
try to over-simplify or play down the complexity of

cases. Instead it sets out the different elements which a successful policy should contain in order to be able to deal with, and ideally prevent, racial harassment.

Who the guide is for

This guide is for anyone working in the housing field who is concerned about racial harassment and is committed to dealing with any incidents of harassment. The guidance given here is equally relevant to housing associations and housing departments of local authorities.

The guide is aimed at policy makers formulating or reviewing their organisation's approach to racial harassment and looking for suggestions of good practice. These policy makers may include senior managers, line managers or housing association committee members and local councillors.

The guide can also be used by staff who have not yet had experience of dealing with racial harassment but may be called upon to do so as part of their job as well as by staff who have in the past handled or who are currently handling cases.

Managers and trainers will also find the guide helpful in presenting and summarising policies and procedures for dealing with racial harassment on training courses.

CHAPTER 1

EXTENT AND DEFINITION OF RACIAL HARASSMENT

Extent of racial harassment

Racial harassment is not a new problem. Attacks on black people occurred at the beginning of this century in many of the dock areas of Britain including Cardiff, Liverpool, Manchester and Hull. Racial attacks have grown since 1945, from riots by members of the white community in London during the late 1950s, 'paki-bashing' in the 1960s, through to the present-day racially motivated physical and verbal attacks, some of which are organised by extreme right-wing groups.

During the 1980s there was official recognition of the increasing scale and numbers of attacks. In 1981 the Commission for Racial Equality (CRE) published the report *Racial Harassment on Local Authority Housing Estates* and in the same year the Home Office produced its own report, *Racial Attacks*. A Home Affairs Committee convened to consider the problem in 1986 stated in *Racial Attacks and Harassment* that 'the most shameful and dispiriting aspect of race relations in Britain is the incidence of racial attacks and harassment'.

The Commission for Racial Equality's report on racial harassment *Living in Terror* was published in 1987. It pointed out that racial harassment did not just occur in areas where there were several black families. Isolated black families were at risk too. The Runnymede Trust in *Racial Violence and Harassment* (1986) underlined the geographical spread of the problem : 'few areas in Britain can now be regarded as safe for black residents . . . racial attacks have taken place in areas such as middle-class Hendon, in Finchley and in Shrewsbury in rural Shropshire.'

Two reports published in 1993 – *Room for All: Tenants' Associations and Race Equality* by the CRE and the Federation of Black Housing Organisations' *Housing Black and Minority Ethnic Elders* – confirmed that racial harassment today is not confined to inner city estates. Rural areas, sheltered housing for the elderly and shared housing, for example, have all been affected.

There is a wide disparity between the officially estimated number of racial attacks and their reporting to the police. In 1993 the minister of state at the Home Office, told the House of Commons home affairs select committee that, based on the British Crime Survey which took account of the level of unreported crime, the annual total of racial attacks could be between 130,000 and 140,000, although in the minister's judgment 'only a minority are serious acts of violence'. This far exceeded any previous estimates of the problem, but may still not reflect the whole picture. By comparison with these official estimates there were 7,793 race attacks actually reported to the police in 1992, down by 89 on 1991.

When the problem has been more intensively and locally researched, its true extent and severity has been uncovered. In *Harassment in London* (1993), a report by the London Research Centre, it was found that 48,000 black and ethnic minority households – or one in 14 of all such households in the capital – had experienced racial harassment in or near their present home. In addition, 16,000 of these households still felt under threat of further racial harassment. Fifty-seven per cent of the households which had been harassed reported this to the authorities, primarily their landlord or community organisation.

Statistics provided by local bodies, such as the Tower Hamlets Law Centre, also point to high levels of harassment but under-reporting to the landlord. The law centre recorded 496 incidents ranging from verbal abuse to major assaults on Bengali and Somali families between 1990 and 1992 on one estate alone. A support group on the Teviot Estate in Tower Hamlets had 370 incidents of racial harassment reported to it during the 12 months from September 1990 to September 1991. By comparison, in the same period, figures from the local authority housing office showed only 83 incidents reported from the same estate. (See *London Housing Statistics 1991* chapter 8, London Research Centre, 1992).

The growing number of deaths attributable to racist violence underlines the need for urgency. Six people were murdered in racist attacks during the first nine months of 1992: four were from the Indian sub-continent, one was a Tamil and one from Afghanistan. Somali people were attacked in Sheffield, Hounslow and

Southall in west London, and Tower Hamlets and Newham in east London. Other serious attacks in 1992 took place in Manchester, Rochdale, Birmingham, Walsall and south London. In 1993 Stephen Lawrence, an 18-year-old youth, whilst waiting at a bus stop in Greenwich was murdered in the street by a group of white youths.

General definition and examples

The law does not define 'racial harassment'. However, the CRE produced a definition in 1987 which remains the basis for developing effective policies to deal with racial harassment.

In *Living in Terror*, the Commission states that racial harassment is:

> Violence which may be verbal or physical and which includes attacks on property as well as on the person, suffered by individuals or groups because of their colour, race, nationality or ethnic or national origins, when the victim believes that the perpetrator was acting on racial grounds, or there is evidence of racism.

Table 1 Definition of racial harassment: key points

1 The importance of taking into account the perception of the person experiencing the harassment in deciding whether or not an incident is racially motivated.

2 Harassment includes verbal and written abuse, as well as physical assault.

> 3 Even if the person experiencing the attack does not mention a racial motive, the person to whom the incident is reported should consider whether there is evidence of such a motive.

The elements set out in Table 1 above are also present in the definition of racial harassment produced in the First Report of the Inter-Departmental Racial Attacks Group:

> Any incident in which it appears to the reporting or investigating officer that the complaint involves an element of racial motivation, or any incident which includes an allegation of racial motivation made by any person. (See *The Response to Racial Attacks and Harassment*, paragraph 14, Home Office, 1989.)

The CRE definition has also been used by the National Federation of Housing Associations in *Racial Harassment: Policies and Procedures for Housing Associations* (1989) and the Association of Metropolitan Authorities' guide *Racial Harassment* (1987).

As described in Chapter 2 below, other landlords, taking the CRE definition as their starting point, have tried to simplify the wording to get the message across to tenants. A clear definition is an important part of having a successful policy for dealing with racial harassment. Many landlords back up their general definition by giving examples of racial harassment. The following list is illustrative but not exhaustive:

1 Threats to the person

— unprovoked physical assaults

— threatening or abusive letters and telephone calls

— verbal abuse, including name calling and swearing

— repeated and unfounded or trivial complaints against a tenant or group of tenants

— threatening or abusive behaviour, including spitting

— failure to control dogs.

2 Damage to the home

— vandalism to property

— graffiti

— arson or attempted arson, including pushing litter or flammable material through doors or windows

— 'flooding out' properties intentionally

— activities intended to deter a person from occupying a particular dwelling, such as hostile 'reception parties'.

3 Harassment outside the home

— placing excrement or rubbish near or in homes

— placing offensive items near homes, for example, putting pigs' heads or feet near Muslim households

— damage to property used by a particular group, including places of worship or community centres or shops

— vandalism of vehicles

— attacks on shops or businesses.

Complainants and perpetrators

Racial harassment in Britain is usually, though obviously not exclusively, aimed at black and other ethnic minority communities. It is mostly carried out by white people. The widespread and well-documented racial discrimination in British society from which many black and other ethnic minority people suffer, however, means that their experience of harassment is significantly different from white people's. The body of data collected by the CRE in *Living in Terror* revealed that racial harassment:

> is an issue where white people are responsible for attacking, in one way or another, people from black and ethnic communities . . . racial attacks and harassment are . . . a 'white problem', with the types of views propagated by extreme right-wing groups being common features of these attacks.

The Home Office report *Racial Attacks* (1981) found that nationwide, Asian people were 50 times more likely than white people to be the victims of racially motivated crimes. Statistics published by the Metropolitan Police show that in 1991, 58 per cent of the racially motivated incidents reported to them were against Indian or Pakistani people and 23 per cent were against African or Afro-caribbean people. In other words, over 80 per cent of the incidents reported to the police in London were against black people.

People who experience harassment include tenants and prospective tenants, or tenants' visitors. Children and women are particularly vulnerable to racial harassment and attacks. White partners of black or ethnic minority people are also frequent targets.

Perpetrators may be neighbours. They may come from off the estate where the harassment is taking place, or they may be from another local area. Most racial attacks involving households on estates are either on isolated black families living on predominantly white estates, or attacks on families living on estates which house many black families where the harassment is carried out by people from outside the estate.

Research by the Policy Studies Institute in 1984 indicates that perpetrators are often white youths: 'the typical perpetrator is a white teenager, often part of a gang and sometimes encouraged by parents.' In 1992 Birmingham City Council was, for example, granted possession against a white couple whose sixteen-year-old son racially abused and attacked a Punjabi woman neighbour for two years. In cases of harassment by minors, the tenant is held responsible for any breaches of the tenancy agreement by their children under the age of 18 who are resident in the property. In addition, tenants are responsible for the actions of their visitors (see also Chapter 5).

In short, racial harassment is defined by the motives of the largely white attackers as perceived by their predominantly black and ethnic minority targets. Attacks are often not reported and so redress for the person who experienced the attack and action against the perpetrator is frequently inadequate.

CHAPTER 2

RACIAL HARASSMENT POLICY ESSENTIALS

Introduction

The CRE's code of practice in rented housing (1991) recommends that all landlords should adopt policies and procedures to deal with racial harassment. In *Room for All* (1993), a CRE survey showed that over 95 per cent of London boroughs and city councils had such policies. *Are You Doing Enough?*, a survey published by the NFHA in 1992, found that 81 per cent of 141 housing associations responding to their questionnaire had already adopted a racial harassment policy or were preparing to do so.

In its code of practice the CRE identified the key elements which a policy for dealing with racial harassment should cover and these points are set out in Table 2.

Table 2 Racial harassment policy: key points

1 A definition of racial harassment
2 Support for people experiencing harassment

> 3 Action against perpetrators
> 4 Working with other agencies
> 5 Preventative action
> 6 Monitoring

Above all tackling racial harassment requires action to support those experiencing the harassment and action against perpetrators. Without this, policies and procedures will be 'little more than a collection of good intentions set down on paper,' as David Yardley, the local government ombudsman observed in reporting on an investigation into the London Borough of Tower Hamlets in 1993. Nonetheless clear policies are as essential in this area as they are for any of the organisation's key responsibilities (see Appendix 1).

Recommended provisions

In *Housing Associations and Racial Equality*, the CRE identified in more detail the elements which a housing association's racial harassment policy should include. Although these standards refer explicitly to housing associations, they, together with the addition of taking preventative action discussed in Chapter 6 below, form the essential elements of any landlord's racial harassment policy. Each of these key elements which follow is discussed in this guide.

— A clear definition of racial harassment (see below)

— A 'no racial harassment' clause in tenancy agreements (see Chapter 6)

— Adoption of a formal procedure to investigate incidents (see Chapters 3 and 8)

— Staff and tenants should be made aware of the policy (see Chapter 7)

— Staff and committee members should be given appropriate training on the policy (see Chapter 9)

— A clear commitment to investigate all reported incidents and to do so as quickly as is practical (see Chapter 3)

— Appointment of a designated officer responsible for investigating incidents (see Chapter 3)

— A clear commitment to support those experiencing racial harassment (see Chapter 4)

— Clear and detailed record keeping of all incidents (see Chapters 3 and 8 and Appendices)

— A clear commitment to take action against perpetrators including, where appropriate, legal proceedings seeking injunctions or orders for possession (see Chapter 5)

— A commitment to take the wishes of the victim fully into account when action is being considered (see Chapters 3 and 4)

— The landlord's solicitors should be informed of incidents and be aware of the relevant statutes (see Chapter 5)

— Incidents of racial harassment should be reported to the police and, where appropriate, the local authority (see Chapters 3, 4, 6 and 8)

— Landlords should participate in any local racial harassment multi-agency forum (see Chapters 4, 6 and 8)

— Statistical reports provided to the management committee on at least a six monthly basis (see Chapters 3 and 8)

— Appointment of a senior officer with overall responsibility for the policy (see Chapter 3)

— A commitment to review the policy and its procedures at least every three years (see Chapter 10).

Formulating a definition

The importance of having a clear definition cannot be over stressed. One perceived difficulty in implementing a racial harassment policy may be that some incidents of racial harassment cannot be distinguished from neighbour disputes. Many racial harassment cases are treated as neighbour disputes because the alleged perpetrator makes a counter charge against the person who made the original report of harassment. In such cases, a different investigating officer should be asked to investigate the counter-claim. If an organisation's definition of racial harassment is such that a key factor in deciding the cause of an incident is whether the person experiencing the harassment believes there is a racial motive for the harassment, this will help distinguish racial harassment from neighbour disputes.

In other circumstances nuisance might be caused unintentionally – a particular form of behaviour which was not designed to give offence or upset having that impact. Noise would be the most obvious example of this. The key distinction here between nuisance and harassment is that the unwanted behaviour is an attack. It is deliberate.

As previously mentioned, it is good practice to include in any definition of racial harassment the following key factors:

— the perception of the person experiencing the harassment as to whether an attack is racially motivated is taken into account

— harassment includes verbal and therefore written abuse, as well as physical assault

— even if the person experiencing the harassment does not mention a racial motive, the person to whom the incident is reported should consider whether there is evidence of such a motive.

Some landlords have sought a simpler and more readable definition which reflects these principles. For example, in its racial harassment policy and procedure guidelines made in 1992, the London Borough of Lambeth gives a definition in these terms:

Racial harassment is when someone intimidates or abuses you, or your family, because of your race, skin colour, nationality, ethnicity or religious belief. This includes acts such as racist name calling, physical attacks, damage to property, racist graffiti and arson.

London Borough of Ealing housing services department produced the following definition in 1991:

Racial harassment is a deliberate act against people, because of their racial origin, which disturbs their peace and comfort. It may be a physical attack but also includes verbal abuse and racist graffiti.

It is good practice to start with the CRE's definition when constructing the policy. Landlords may however consider using a simpler and more accessible form of words, along the lines of the examples quoted above, for publicising the policy, training and guiding their staff and when interviewing people experiencing harassment or suspected perpetrators.

One note of caution needs to be struck on defining racial harassment. Anxieties or confusion about definitions should not delay or become a substitute for action to stop the unwanted and unacceptable behaviour, support the person experiencing the harassment, and take action against the perpetrator. Duncan Forbes and Lee Bridges give a salutary warning in *Making the Law Work on Racial Harassment* (1991) 'Some authorities spent many months attempting to establish whether harassment which was quite definitely occurring was racially motivated. By the time a decision was made, no action could be taken even if it was racial. In any event immediate action should have been taken to deal with the harassment, regardless of its motive.'

CHAPTER 3

INVESTIGATING INCIDENTS OF RACIAL HARASSMENT

Reports of incidents

Incidents of racial harassment may come to the landlord's notice in a wide variety of ways. Some may be reported by people experiencing harassment directly to housing officers or other staff, including caretakers, cleaners, maintenance staff and wardens. Incidents also may be reported to the landlord by the police or other agencies such as a local authority social services departments, schools, advice agencies or by community organisations. Friends or neighbours of people who have been harassed may report incidents, or staff themselves may see evidence, for example, graffiti. Regardless of the source, it is good practice to follow the same procedure once a report of an incident has been received.

Many incidents will first come to light as a request for a housing transfer or a request for maintenance work. In the case of transfer requests, acts of racial harassment are likely to have been taking place over an extended period of time. It will take considerable frustration and despair of the harassment stopping before a tenant seeks to voluntarily give up their home.

Some housing managers have expressed concern that tenants may spuriously complain of racial harassment in order to gain priority for a transfer. Whilst this is theoretically possible, there is little evidence of the practice. On the contrary, the evidence, as shown in Chapter 1, is of considerable under-reporting of racial harassment.

When dealing with maintenance requests, staff will need to be vigilant about ensuring that they do not unwittingly ignore harassment which may be causing considerable distress to tenants.

At the beginning, reported acts of racial harassment should be referred for investigation to a neighbourhood housing officer, an estate officer, area management officer or another appropriate named officer. That person is referred to as the 'investigating officer' in this guide. The investigating officer should be the member of staff normally responsible for managing the tenancy of the person experiencing the harassment. This referral must be done immediately if there has been violence, or otherwise within 24 hours.

The person being harassed may themselves sometimes identify a racial motive, and this will dictate that the incident is investigated as one of racial harassment. In other cases it will be for the member of staff receiving the report to decide whether to follow the racial harassment procedure. As already stated, there will be instances when the person who receives the initial report may not be a member of the housing staff. They may be, for example, receptionists, administrators, maintenance officers or surveyors. In these circumstances all the staff mentioned will have to consider whether to invoke the racial harassment policy. (An example of a racial harassment policy is included in Appendix 1). When thinking about this they will have to take into account, for example, has there been obvious evidence of a racial motive, such as words used? Are there any other indications which might suggest a racial motive – do the attacks seem to be premeditated or recurrent, for instance?

It is good practice to include such examples in the guidelines given to staff to enable them to decide whether an incident should be dealt with under the racial harassment policy. If in doubt, it is better to err on the side of safety and follow the racial harassment procedure. Experience has shown that racial harassment can escalate quickly if incidents are ignored: the welfare of the person experiencing harassment must be safeguarded and be the primary consideration.

Staff who may receive reports of harassment but will not be the investigating officer should also be included in training on racial harassment. This is covered in more detail in Chapter 9.

Starting the investigation

Whenever an incident is reported, it is good practice to arrange an initial interview at once if violence is involved; if not, within 24 hours, or, should a weekend intervene, the next working day at the latest. Since incidents of harassment may occur at weekends or at night, this means that provision must be made for staff who are familiar with the racial harassment procedures to be available on emergency call, and for frontline staff such as caretakers and wardens to know how to reach such staff, and themselves to be able to offer some immediate support if necessary. Recognising this, many landlords have established 24-hour helplines for people experiencing harassment. In addition, all frontline staff need to be aware of the guidelines about collecting evidence discussed below.

A case file alongside the tenancy file should be set up by the investigating officer immediately to record all reported details and any action taken. Details about the administrative systems and procedures needed to back up the policy follow in Chapter 8.

At this early stage of the procedure, the officer investigating the incident will not know whether legal proceedings will be instigated. The officer should there-fore collect all available evidence as carefully as possible even though in most cases there may be no eventual legal action. This is best done through the use of standard forms, examples of which are given in the Appendices 2–7.

Initial interview

The first interview with a person experiencing racial harassment will be vital in determining the landlord's response. That interview has two main objectives. First, to convince that person – who may well be frightened and confused as well as sceptical about the landlord's attitude and commitment – that the organisation takes harassment very seriously and is keen to prevent and stop it. The organisation's commitment to act in accord-ance with the wishes, and in the best interests of the person experiencing harassment needs to be made clear, together with the landlord's firm intention to take action against the perpetrator, where possible and appropriate, with the consent of the person being harassed. Secondly, the investigating officer will want to make an accurate record of all incidents of racial harassment to date.

Careful preparation for the initial interview is essential and this should include:

— arranging a convenient time and place for the interview

— clarifying the purpose of the interview

— obtaining any necessary forms, leaflets or other information

— obtaining briefing on the case to date from other staff, or written records

— anticipating likely questions and possible answers.

Interpreters

Some interviewees will not be fluent in English and should therefore be interviewed in their own language. Ideally, a landlord will already employ bi-lingual staff who can conduct such interviews. The good landlord will also have a record of the first language of all of their tenants. If this information is not readily available from tenancy files, it should definitely be established before the interview.

It is good practice, at the very least, to have available up-to-date lists of interpreters, and an established procedure which allows staff to contact an interpreter quickly if necessary, unfettered by the rigours of the expenditure authorisation system, or some other bureaucratic hurdle. It is also good practice to ensure that interpreters are aware of the sensitivity and, most importantly, confidentiality of the cases in which they may be involved.

Children should not be used as interpreters. The material they will be asked to convey may well be disturbing and complex. It is not fair either to them, or to the person being harassed, that this onerous responsibility should fall on one who may be unable to understand or bear the weight.

Community agencies may also be inappropriate. Whilst they may be willing and helpful advocates and interpreters, they are often legitimately concerned with wider campaigns and may see each case through that filter. The urge to campaign may not square with the understandable desire of the person being harassed to keep their problems anonymous and confidential. Their main objective is likely to be stopping the harassment they are experiencing. Wider community campaigns may be at best a secondary concern.

Women could be given the choice of being interviewed by a female member of staff. This should be offered, rather than only agreed to if the person being harassed raises the point. This option should not just be available in office hours. It also needs to be incorporated in the emergency contact provisions mentioned above.

Some people being harassed may wish to have a friend or relative with them during the interview. This should be acceptable, unless it is disruptive. It may be that the relative or friend is the person most trusted by the person experiencing the harassment, and they will therefore be effective interpreters. However, it may also be the case that they are not interpreting, but advocating. Whilst this could very well be in the best interest of the person being harassed, it may also be necessary to have an independent interpreter who could translate objectively.

Taking notes

Compiling accurate and complete notes of the interview is essential good practice. Even if an incident appears minor, full details should be written up. A case against one offender will be stronger if several people who have experienced harassment in their homes give evidence.

As shown in the specimen report form for visits to those experiencing harassment in Appendix 3, a detailed description of the incident is required. This should include, for example, details of the date, time and location of the incident, the nature of the assault, damage, words used, the identity or description of the perpetrator, and the names and addresses of any witnesses. The investigating officer will need to write down possible witnesses' names, addresses and phone numbers and interview them as soon as possible. The person being harassed will need to check that the details recorded are correct before both interviewer and interviewee sign the form.

It is important to get the interviewee's agreement to the interviewer taking notes. This will require an explanation of what the notes will contain, and to what purpose they will be put. Care should be taken to avoid the note-taking being experienced by the interviewee as intimidating, bureaucratic or insensitive.

Any personal injuries should be carefully described and, if possible, photographed and a record kept of the date and the person taking the pictures. A camera and film should be readily accessible.

Table 3 below provides guidelines for staff when conducting the first interview of a person who has experienced racial harassment.

Table 3 Initial interview: key points

1 Believe what they are saying

2 Do not question their motives

3 Arrange interpreters/any other necessary assistance with communication. Do not expect person being harassed to make these arrangements

4 Encourage them to have a friend, relative or supporter present if that is helpful

5 Allow them the time to express themselves

6 Assure them of your support

7 Explain the landlord's policy of support for people being harassed and action against perpetrators

8 Assure them of confidentiality

9 Explain why you need to take notes

10 Note down as closely as possible what is said, not your interpretation

11 Show them notes to verify. Read back if necessary

12 Be prepared to make a second visit

13 Take photographs of any evidence

14 Discuss practical and emotional support needed

15 Seek their consent for the next steps

16 Agree time and place for follow-up discussion.

Next steps

Attention should also be given to the action that is immediately necessary after the initial interview, which includes:

— writing notes

— sending any necessary letters

— completing forms

— carrying out any other steps agreed with the person experiencing harassment

— checking or monitoring to ensure that follow-up action by others has been completed

— ensuring that office records are up-to-date.

The investigating officer should compile their report using a standard format as suggested in Appendix 3 within two working days of completing the initial interview. This report should be considered by their line manager or any other appropriate senior officers within a maximum of two working days of its receipt. Some housing providers convene a panel or working party to consider the report. The panel consists of the investigating officer and the appropriate senior officer. However, panels sometimes are not able to make decisions quickly enough. It may be more appropriate to use a panel for monitoring the progress on cases, and for line managers to take responsibility for day-to-day decisions on cases. (See Appendix 12 for suggested terms of reference for racial harassment working parties).

It is good practice for the investigating officer's report to contain details of action taken to date and recommendations for any future action. It should also contain deadlines for decisions recommended to be implemented.

When the appropriate manager or panel reaches a decision on action to be taken, this should be recorded on the case file. The main options for further action are set out below:

— collect more details on case; more witnesses; contact other agencies (see Chapter 4)

— no immediate action apart from monitoring situation, for example, via regular visits (see also Chapter 8)

— visit the perpetrator and try to stop the harassment (see below)

— involve the police in taking action against perpetrator (see below)

— provide practical and emotional support (see Chapter 4)

— start legal action against perpetrator (see Chapter 5)

— recommend temporary or permanent rehousing (see Chapter 4).

If the person experiencing harassment is currently in temporary accommodation the main options for further action are:

— visit to monitor situation (see also Chapter 8)

— consider move to other temporary accommodation for person being harassed or perpetrator (see Chapter 4)

— prioritise the assessment and/or rehousing of the complainant (see Chapter 4)

— collect more information and contact other agencies and residents (see Chapter 4)

— visit perpetrator and try to stop the harassment (see below)

— start legal proceedings against perpetrator (see Chapter 5)

— involve the police in taking action against perpetrator (see below and also Chapter 5)

— ensure that no hostels are used where there has been proven harassment by hostel owners or staff members (see also Chapter 5).

If the person being harassed is currently resident in a property which is part of a short-life co-op, the available options are:

— find alternative short-life property for person being harassed or the perpetrator (see also Chapter 4)

— take back licences from the perpetrator if appropriate

— consider withdrawing approval and housing from an individual co-op.

These are the options if the person being harassed is a tenant of a private landlord:

— refer to police (see below and Chapter 5)

— refer case to local authority social services (see Chapter 5)

— in some circumstances people being harassed may be eligible for rehousing by local authorities if they have been rendered homeless because of the harassment (see Chapter 4)

— offer legal advice on protection from eviction.

Detailed guidance on interviewing and supporting those experiencing harassment is given in a companion volume to this series to be published in 1994 – *Support for People Experiencing Racial Harassment.*

Contacting the police

It is impossible for landlords to handle the problem of racial harassment alone. Many incidents happen outside the home; in some cases the perpetrator and the person being harassed are not tenants of the same landlord; in cases of criminal damage or assault, the police may be the best or only authority able to act against perpetrators (see Chapter 5). The police have become increasingly aware of the scale and severity of the problem and are nationally committed to tackling racial harassment, although this has not always been the experience at local level.

Some forces have set up specialist teams of officers to deal with racial attacks. They can be expected to be better informed and more sympathetic. Landlords will need to seek them out when reporting a case, particularly if there has been no previous contact with a police station.

A racial harassment policy must therefore include guidance about contacting the police, particularly specialist officers, and working with them. A person being harassed may have already told the police. If not, the investigating housing officer should do so on that person's behalf, or together with them if that is preferred by the person who has been harassed. The consent of the person being harassed should be obtained before an approach is made to the police. This consent should be recorded on the file, together with notes made of any conversation with the police.

It is important to maintain contact with the police about their work on the case, especially if they are taking the lead in identifying or dealing with the perpetrator. It might also be helpful to meet regularly with beat officers and specialist racial attacks teams to co-ordinate strategies for prevention and protection over an entire area. Dealing with each case individually may obscure or hide patterns of escalation.

People being harassed may be reluctant to contact the police. This may be because they fear further repercussions from the perpetrators if the police are involved, or because they have no confidence that the police will take the incident seriously or deal with the matter effectively. The investigating housing officer will need to spend time discovering the reasons for any reluctance to contact the police and allay any unjustified fears. Some of these fears may also be mitigated by contact with sympathetic specialist police officers. If possible, these officers may be able to provide anonymous examples of where the police have made a positive contribution to the resolution of a racial harassment case.

Staff should stress that the police are anxious to co-operate (if that is locally the case) and are sometimes better placed to stop further harassment than the landlord. The involvement of the police does not necess-arily mean that a victim will have to appear in court. The police may deal with a case by a formal caution to an individual perpetrator or a general warning to all those who may be involved in the neighbourhood, or they could increase their presence in a certain area.

Where the person being harassed remains adamant that there should be no approach to the police, this should not be viewed as a weakness in their complaint, nor result in the case being pursued less vigorously, or being closed altogether.

The investigating housing officer may decide in an exceptional case that an approach must be made to the police, even though the person being harassed has not given their consent. Such cases might include instances when staff fear for the physical safety of that person. An approach to the police in these circumstances must be agreed by the most senior housing officer responsible for the implementation of the racial harassment policy, and the reasons for the decision recorded. The police may decide to pursue the case against the perpetrator and will need to be aware that their involvement has been sought without the consent of the person being harassed. They will, therefore, need to gain the trust of the person being harassed. In some instances the landlord will be able to help in this regard.

CHAPTER 4

SUPPORTING PEOPLE EXPERIENCING RACIAL HARASSMENT

Introduction

Initial support may be of a personal nature – comforting and reassuring a person experiencing harassment. All staff, including caretakers and wardens, should be trained to offer positive reassurance to a person being harassed that their complaint will be investigated and that they will be protected and supported, without making unachievable promises of specific action, such as an immediate transfer.

Other means of emotional support could include contacting friends or relatives or a community organisation. It is good practice to ensure that lists of support organisations are regularly updated and readily available to both the investigating officer and the person being harassed. There may also be other forms of practical support that should be offered, for example, ensuring that maintenance work is done as a matter of urgency and providing phone numbers and addresses of agencies offering support out of office hours. Table 4 below sets out the key aspects of supporting people who have experienced racial harassment.

Table 4 Support for people being harassed: key points

1 Offer reassurance and support
2 Refer to community organisations for support
3 Ensure maintenance works are done as a priority
4 Consider the provision of additional security works
5 Ensure that estate based housing staff are known to the tenant
6 Provide person being harassed with telephone numbers and addresses of emergency services and other agencies offering support out of office hours
7 Ensure person being harassed knows how to contact investigating officer
8 Ensure person being harassed is clear on next steps to be taken
9 Consider giving personal alarms to people experiencing harassment
10 Link up to helpline, installing telephone if necessary.

Contact with other agencies

There is widespread recognition of the need for the problem of racial harassment to be fought on many fronts – a multi-agency approach. The government's inter-departmental initiatives have resulted in police, housing services, social services, education services,

probation service, and community organisations beginning to identify ways in which they can work together
to tackle harassment. (See generally *The Response to Racial
Attacks: Sustaining the Momentum*, Home Office, 1991).

At a strategic level, housing providers need to be
involved with any local multi-agency initiatives (see
Chapter 6). Operationally, housing providers will need
contacts with the social services and the education
service in particular to deal with cases effectively. For
example, harassment may continue against children and
young people in the street, the playground or the class
room. Teachers can be an important focus of authority
and therefore the means of stopping the harassment. In
addition, many schools have their own policies and
guidelines for tackling racial harassment. Social
workers can be an important link in the support
network that those experiencing harassment will need.
Other agencies may be able to offer support to the
person being harassed and their family, as well as
collecting evidence.

Organisations need to maintain up-to-date lists of
clearly identified contacts within local social services
and the local education and youth services, including
local schools.

Keeping in touch

At the initial interview, the investigating officer should
discuss with the complainant the best way of keeping in
touch. Some housing providers, such as Leicester City
Council housing department have issued complainants
with alarms connected to their 'careline' centres. This
enables people who have been harassed to make instant

contact with emergency and other support services when another incident occurs. Other approaches are to provide diary sheets to log any further incidents. An example is included in Appendix 7. Some complainants may prefer to use a cassette tape recorder as a diary, or a camera to photograph evidence. In all cases those experiencing the harassment should be given relevant phone numbers for any emergency contacts, and a timetable for investigating the case, including when the victim can expect to hear again from the investigating officer.

Local housing staff, especially caretakers, have an important part to play in keeping in touch with victims, and watching for any re-occurrence of harassment.

Repairs to property

Different housing providers have different timescales for dealing with repairs arising from racial harassment. Table 5 sets out recommended response times for effecting repairs.

Table 5 Recommended response times for repairs

1 Any repairs that are needed to make a property secure and safe should be treated as emergency repairs and carried out within 12 hours.

2 Other repairs arising from racial harassment should be carried out within 72 hours.

3 Racist graffiti, stickers or posters should be removed within 24 hours if they occur in or around a particular tenant's home and within 72 hours if in a public area.

Damage to property or racist graffiti linked with racial harassment should be photographed before a repair is carried out or the offensive graffiti removed.

The investigating officer should record the costs of any repairs, and if possible charge the cost to the perpetrator.

A report to the police must include details of damage to property. In order to investigate an offence under the Criminal Damage Act 1971 the police may well want to visit the person experiencing the harassment, so it is important that they are forewarned.

Some housing providers have a policy that damage not reported to the police must be paid for by the tenant. In cases of racial harassment, however, if the victim does not want to make a report to the police, this should not mean that any damage should be paid for by them.

Temporary accommodation

It is not good practice to respond to racial harassment by rehousing victims automatically. This action may only encourage the perpetrators to attempt to drive out more people by harassing them.

There may be occasions when people are concerned by the prospect of actual or threatened physical assault and so are afraid to go back to their home. In these cases, the landlord may wish to provide temporary accommodation while the case is being investigated. A decision to provide temporary accommodation must be taken at the most senior management level. The decision should be taken in the context of re-affirming the tenant's right to live in their own home in peace. The duty of the landlord is to ensure that they can. Temporary accommodation should only be seen as a staging post in achieving that objective. While the tenant is away the landlord and other agencies should seek to end the harassment, and remove the potential for it recurring, and then move the tenant back.

Where the decision is taken to move the person experiencing harassment to temporary accommodation, the move should cause as little disruption as possible to their household. The costs of the move should be borne by the landlord, as the tenant has not moved of their own volition.

Moving to temporary accommodation should not be seen as an end to the landlord's responsibility. Nor should it be seen as a precursor to an inexorable permanent move.

Rehousing

As noted above, moving the person being harassed is rarely the best option. It may seem like a victory for the harasser, and creates a management problem for the landlord when it comes to re-letting the property. Rehousing may also create disruption for the family of the person being harassed, breaking up any local support from relatives, friends and community which the household may have and enforcing other changes, such as in schools.

However, it should not be part of a racial harassment policy to turn households into martyrs or allow them to be targets for attacks. If all other avenues have been explored and have failed to lead to a solution, and the tenants being harassed feel unable to continue to live in their current home, the landlord may decide that rehousing is the best or only option.

The 1991 Code of Guidance for local authorities on homelessness (paragraph 6.17) states that authorities should consider applications from 'those at risk of harassment or violence on account of their gender, race, colour, ethnic or national origin.' People experiencing racial violence may therefore be treated either as homeless, particularly if they are not current tenants, or as management transfers if they are currently tenants, and re-housed accordingly.

If a racial harassment case is to be dealt with through a management transfer, it is good practice to ensure that the usual constraints that apply to management transfers, such as the ineligibility of tenants with rent arrears are not unreasonably applied. This should also cover such matters as length of residence in a property. In addition, within the limits of available property, the person being harassed should be offered a property that is at least equal in quality to the current one. The views of the person being harassed with regard to location should be taken into account as far as possible.

It may take some months before the process of rehousing is completed. Staff should continue to provide support and protection, together with other agencies, until rehousing occurs.

The housing officer responsible for the former property should have made contact with all appropriate support agencies at the new address to provide on-going support. Once a household is rehoused, they may still need support to help them feel safe in their new surroundings. Good practice in dealing with cases of racial harassment includes arranging for continuing support from whatever is the most appropriate source, for as long as it is needed. Even if the landlord is not the main provider of this support, which may come from a community organisation for example, the local housing officers should be responsible for ensuring that such support is delivered.

The local housing staff at the new property, particularly estate based staff such as caretakers, should maintain contact with the household for the first few months, and report any cause for concern.

People being harassed may need assistance with transfer expenses for removals and connection and reconnection of appliances and telephone. They may also need assistance in arranging for these tasks to be completed, particularly if English is not their first language. Assistance from the landlord's representative with these matters will, apart from helping with the immediate tasks in hand, also reinforce the message that the landlord is serious about dealing with racial harassment, and will provide the necessary support.

Even if a person being harassed is rehoused, responsibility remains for investigating the original incident. In particular, the landlord will want to monitor whether there is any recurrence of harassment.

Letting vacated property

When someone moves because of racial harassment perpetrators may think they have proved a point if the property is then let to a white household. If the property is let to a black or ethnic minority family, this will demonstrate that the perpetrators have not won, and that the landlord is not content to collude in the creation of areas for white people only. However a black household who moves into a property vacated through racial harassment may themselves face harassment. Table 6 below sets out good practice on letting vacated properties.

Table 6 Letting vacated property: key points

1 Offer the property using standard procedures - do not make a formal or informal decision not to offer the property to another black or ethnic minority family.

2 If the property is offered to a black or ethnic minority household through the normal procedure, explain the history of the property and the steps the landlord is taking to deal with the problem. If the household decides to turn down the offer, this should not count as a refusal of a formal offer.

3 If the household decides to accept the property, the local housing staff should ensure that they keep in regular and frequent touch with the household for the first few months. If any harassment occurs, prompt action should be taken. There should be liaison with local statutory and voluntary agencies, including tenants' associations, to support the household.

4 Bear in mind the vulnerability of isolated black and other ethnic minority households on mainly white estates, and ensure that where possible black and other ethnic minority tenants are not exposed to such isolation. This does not mean that all black tenants should be housed together, but rather that black households' expressed perceptions of where they feel safe should be taken into account in lettings as far as possible.

CHAPTER 5

ACTION AGAINST PERPETRATORS

Introduction

Effective action against perpetrators is an essential part of a strategy for combatting racial harassment. Being seen to take action against offenders will make it clear that such behaviour is not tolerated, an important message to the perpetrator, other putative attackers, as well as to other tenants who are experiencing harassment but have previously been reluctant to report it.

It is easier to take effective action if the perpetrators can be identified, but this is not always possible. This chapter looks at the options for action available when offenders are known, and also when they are not.

Action should be taken by the police and/or by the landlord, rather than by the person being harassed. A person being harassed can take individual action through the courts themselves but this is generally inadvisable for several reasons. These include difficulties in obtaining legal aid, the additional strain on a person being harassed and the likelihood of a perpetrator making a counter-claim. The usual outcome of such cases is for both parties to be bound over to keep the peace. In any event possession proceedings cannot be instigated by another tenant, whereas if the landlord takes action, an eviction order may be sought and granted.

Landlord's options

The following are the main categories of possible action to be taken by landlords.

First, to issue a formal warning. A formal letter should be sent, referring to the interview (see below) and reminding the tenant of the terms of the tenancy agreement. The letter should explain what action could follow if harassment continues.

Secondly, to charge the offenders for costs. The cost of any repairs or graffiti removal could be charged to the perpetrator. If they refuse, and the landlord considers there is evidence that they are liable, the landlord may wish to refer the matter to the police for investigation (see Chapter 4). Even if the police do not want to prosecute, a landlord may decide to prosecute privately.

Thirdly, to start immediate legal action. Depending on the scale of the harassment and the soundness of the evidence against the perpetrator, the landlord may decide to ask their solicitors or legal department to consider taking legal action to evict or take out private prosecutions for assault or damage if the police do not prosecute (see below).

Interviewing perpetrators

If the person experiencing the harassment agrees, and if

the perpetrator has been identified, the perpetrator should be interviewed as soon as possible by the investigating officer. If they are a tenant of the same landlord it is clearly easier to insist on interviewing them in order to explain the landlord's policy.

If they are tenants of other landlords, or owner occupiers they should still be interviewed so that the potential consequences of their continuing to harass the tenant are explained to them – that they may be criminally prosecuted, or that other forms of legal action may be taken against them.

Essential detailed guidance on this difficult topic is provided in the first book in this series *Interviewing Perpetrators of Racial Harassment*. The key points to be borne in mind at the outset by an investigating officer are:

1 Be clear about the purpose of the interview. This is to:

— inform the suspected perpetrator of a complaint

— explain the landlords' racial harassment policy

— discourage further incidents

— to stop the harassment.

2 The purpose of interviewing a suspected per-petrator is not to:

— accuse the perpetrator

— wring an admission of guilt

— conduct a detective inquiry

— convey the anger of the person being harassed.

3   An interview with a suspected perpetrator should cover four main stages. These are:

— providing an explanation of the incident

— noting and assessing the reaction of the suspected perpetrator

— indicating the possible consequences to the perpetrators of their suspected actions

— outlining the next steps the landlord proposes to take.

Suspected perpetrators may respond in one or more of the following ways. They may deny the accusation; blame someone else; make a counter-accusation; blame the tenant who has been harassed; criticise the landlord for interference; or use threatening behaviour.

A racial harassment procedure should ensure that housing staff never interview suspected perpetrators on their own. If the person being harassed has agreed to the police being notified, a police officer should accompany the housing officer. Otherwise, another housing officer should accompany the investigating officer.

It is good practice to make full notes of any interview. After the interview the relevant officers, with their managers should decide what action to take. This may include collecting statements from other neighbours and witnesses. (See also Appendix 4, 5 and 6).

The investigating officer should also follow up the interview with a letter:

— describing the incidents, but not revealing the identity of the person experiencing the harassment.

— summarising the landlord's policy on harassment.

— quoting the 'no harassment' clause in the tenancy agreement.

— reminding them that persistent harassment could result in the perpetrator losing their home.

— summarising any agreed next steps, for example, that they will seek to prevent their children or visitors committing acts of harassment.

Legal remedies

Landlords may take possession proceedings against tenants who are themselves, or whose families are, committing acts of racial harassment. Even if there is no specific clause in the tenancy agreement prohibiting racial harassment, landlords may take action to evict on ground 2 of schedule 2 to the Housing Act 1985 where 'the tenant or any person living with the tenant has committed a nuisance or annoyance to the neighbours'. Many landlords now include a clause in their tenancy agreement along the lines set out in Chapter 6.

Legal action has been used effectively by several local authorities to tackle racial harassment. In 1993 Leicester District Council evicted a couple who had carried out repeated acts of harassment over several years, including putting up posters saying 'Go back to where you came from'. In the same year Sheffield City Council found that in one case the threat of eviction was sufficient to bring an end to acts of racial harassment. The tenant concerned gave an undertaking to avoid causing 'danger, nuisance or annoyance' when he realised the council was serious in its attempt to evict him for breaching a racial harassment clause in his tenancy agreement. Brighton Borough Council, the London Boroughs of Camden, Ealing, Hammersmith and Fulham, Islington, Newham, Southwark, Tower Hamlets and Greenwich have also successfully taken action.

Amongst housing associations, Family Housing Association in London, New Islington and Hackney Housing Association have been granted possession orders, and Circle 33 Housing Trust has been granted an injunction against a persistent harasser.

Where the landlord is a local authority, there are numerous other legal powers available, although they are much less frequently used. For example, section 222 of the Local Government Act 1972 provides, 'where a local authority considers it expedient for the promotion or protection of the interests of the inhabitants of their area they may prosecute or defend or appear in any legal proceedings and, in the case of civil proceedings, may institute them in their own name.' Duncan Forbes, in his book *Action on Racial Harassment* (1988) notes 'in the context of a racial harassment policy there are at least five uses of section 222 that might be considered by local authorities. They are: prosecutions in criminal proceedings; obtaining injunctions to prevent the commission of criminal offences; obtaining injunctions to prevent public nuisances; obtaining injunctions to prevent the obstruction of an authority's duties; and appearing in proceedings brought by others.'

These and other powers will be discussed in more detail in another title in this series *Legal Remedies for Racial Harassment*. The following two sections on possession proceedings and injunctions provide an outline of what may be gained by those specific forms of action in the courts.

Possession proceedings

To obtain a possession order against a perpetrator of racial harassment, a landlord must:

— serve a notice of seeking possession and give reasons

— establish grounds for possession because of racial harassment

— ensure that the court will consider it reasonable to make a court order

— make sure that the case is strong.

It is important, therefore, that cases are prepared for court with the utmost care. There is some evidence that courts are more likely to grant possession if the perpetrator has committed more than one act of harassment against more than one other tenant. Collecting evidence from everyone who has experienced harassment can be crucial to the success of an individual case.

In Duncan Forbes' and Lee Bridges' *Making the Law*

Work on Racial Harassment (1990) the following stages in possession proceedings are set out:

> Where a complaint is received, a decision should be made as to the appropriate stage at which to commence action against the perpetrator. For example, where incidents are minor, stage 1 may be appropriate in the first instance, with progress to further stages if harassment is repeated. For some serious incidents, it would be appropriate for the initial sanction to be at a more advanced stage, for example, an application for an injunction and service of a notice seeking possession. Where any further racial harassment occurs, subsequent sanctions should be taken at a more advanced stage.

Stage 1   Informal oral warning.

Stage 2   Formal written warning.

Stage 3   Notice of seeking possession with covering warning letter.

Stage 4   Application for permanent injunction restraining breach of tenancy agreement and service of notice seeking possession with warning letter.

Stage 5   Application for interlocutory injunction in proceedings for permanent injunction and service of a notice seeking possession with warning letter.

Stage 6   Service of notice seeking possession; followed by an application for interlocutory injunction restraining breach of tenancy agreement in proceedings for possession, but proceedings adjourned *sine die* after injunction obtained (provided the defendant agrees). Warning letter indicating that proceedings will be continued if further incidents occur.

Stage 7 Application for interlocutory injunction restraining breach of the tenancy agreement, service of notice seeking possession and, when this has expired, a claim for possession at which a suspended possession order is sought.

Stage 8 Application for interlocutory injunction restraining breach of the tenancy agreement, service of notice seeking possession and, when this has expired, a claim for an outright possession order at the earliest possible opportunity.

Stage 9 *Ex parte* application for injunction ordering the defendant out of the premises, followed by an expedited claim for possession.

Injunctions

There are other circumstances in which injunctions may be used in racial harassment cases:

— permanently to prevent perpetrators from repeating acts of harassment, known as a perpetual injunction

— temporarily to prohibit harassment until a possession order is granted, known as an interlocutory injunction

— to stop perpetrators where the landlord has

received advance warning of planned harassment, known as a *quia timet* injunction

— to restrain criminal offences

— to restrain a public nuisance or 'unreasonable use of the highway'. The power to gain this injunction is confined to local authorities

— to prevent an obstruction of a local authority's statutory duty.

In 1993 the London Borough of Southwark was granted injunctions in the High Court against 10 youths accused of racially harassing tenants in the Cherry Gardens of Rotherhithe. They prevented the youths from gathering in the area for the purpose of illegal activities, from assaulting, intimidating or abusing tenants and from causing criminal damage to tenants' or council property.

When the harassment takes place in bed and breakfast accommodation or hostel accommodation, the landlord may obtain an injunction using the Protection from Eviction Act 1977. This statute also enables a housing provider to take action against a private tenant or an owner occupier. Owner occupiers who have bought from the landlord may be in breach of a covenant against causing nuisance contained in the transfer and so action could be taken against them. The London Borough of Southwark took out three injunctions against such Right To Buy leaseholders in 1991 (see *London Housing Statistics*, London Research Centre, 1992).

Intentional homelessness

Where a tenant is evicted for racial harassment, a local authority will have to decide whether the household is intentionally homeless. Each case will have to be investigated but some local authorities make it clear that they will judge anyone evicted for racial harassment as intentionally homeless. If there are no special circumstances as set out in Part III of the Housing Act 1985, then there is no duty on a local authority to rehouse such families.

If a local authority obtains an eviction, it should ensure that the department dealing with homeless households is notified of the order, in case the harassers claim to be homeless. Housing associations, if they evict, should also contact the local authority's homeless unit with the same information. Perpetrators should also be warned that, if they are evicted, they are unlikely to be rehoused by the local authority.

Rehousing perpetrators

In certain circumstances, the landlord may decide to rehouse the perpetrator, even after a possession order has been granted, because the provisions of Part III of the Housing Act 1985 apply. Alternatively, the landlord may secure the perpetrator's agreement to being transferred to prevent legal action, especially where there are fears that the landlord's case is weak. In such a case, the perpetrator should not gain from the transfer in terms of location or quality of accommodation, and the local housing services should be notified of the reason for the transfer.

A landlord may also decide not to apply for eviction if the offender is elderly or vulnerable in some other way. A landlord should take all medical and social factors into account and may decide that an agreement by the perpetrator not to go near the home of the person being harassed will suffice. This could be enforced through an injunction. Where it is not appropriate to take action against a vulnerable perpetrator (see below), and where the perpetrator cannot be moved, rehousing the person experiencing the harassment may be the only option.

Unidentified perpetrators

If a perpetrator cannot be identified, or if a person being harassed is unwilling to identify a suspected perpetrator, there are still a range of possible actions. Again, both the police and the landlord have potential roles to play.

The police can take informal action by giving non-specific warnings to possible perpetrators and by taking a higher profile in the area at times when attacks have occurred. In several cases, the police have visited every flat in a block or on an estate to make it clear that anyone found carrying out an act of harassment would be prosecuted. It usually stops the harassment.

Landlords can take action such as issuing a general warning letter to tenants in one particular area where harassment has occurred, warning of the possible consequences of harassment (see Appendix 8). They may also increase the preventative work described in Chapter 6. Support from tenants' associations may be enlisted to give informal warning advice to possible offenders. If children are involved, head teachers can be

approached by landlords to take up the issue of harassment in school.

Vulnerable perpetrators

In some instances the perpetrators are themselves
vulnerable, for example, they may have histories of
mental health problems. In these cases a judgement will
have to be made about the efficacy of injunctions.
Eviction is unlikely to be an appropriate course of action.
The most suitable action in cases of persistent harassment which does not cease after verbal and written
warnings would be to take proceedings for possession at
the earliest opportunity, coupled with an offer of
suitable alternative accommodation. A possession order
is unlikely to be granted without this offer. In effect, the
landlord is enforcing a compulsory transfer. The
alternative offer will need to be carefully selected in
order to ensure that the problem does not recur.

Action by the police

The police can use a variety of powers to investigate and
bring prosecutions arising out of racial harassment.
Prosecutions may be brought in cases of common
assault (for example, jostling, pushing, throwing stones
through windows); actual bodily harm (for example,
scratching or bruising); and grievous bodily harm (for
example, stabbing, wounding with a knife, an air gun or
brick). Under the Criminal Damage Act 1971 the police
may prosecute people accused of damage to windows
and doors as well as making graffiti or arson attacks.
The Public Order Act 1986 entitles the police to take

action in cases of violent disorder, riot and threatening, abusive or insulting words or behaviour used with the intent to stir up racial hatred.

In addition to charging someone with an offence, in cases where there is insufficient evidence to prosecute, a formal warning or caution from the police to admitted offenders may prevent a repetition of the harassment. This is most often used where the offenders are children.

Action by the Commission for Racial Equality

Sections 20 and 21 of the Race Relations Act 1976 requires that providers of services, including housing, do not discriminate either in access to or in the quality of services. Failure to tackle the racial harassment a tenant is experiencing could therefore be discriminatory and illegal.

Section 31 of the Race Relations Act 1976 makes it illegal to exert pressure to discriminate. Should an individual or a group of tenants seek to prevent a landlord from letting a property to a member of a particular ethnic group, they could be acting unlawfully under this section of the legislation. The CRE used this power in the East End of London in 1984.

Racial harassment and violence had been common on the Exmouth estate in the London Borough of Tower Hamlets. Reports had been received of hostile 'reception committees', serious physical assault and racial abuse. One flat had been vandalised and spray-painted with racist slogans immediately after it had been viewed by an asian family who were being re-housed as a result of persistent racial harassment.

The landlords, the Greater London Council, told the Commission for Racial Equality that a petition had been received from the tenants urging the Council not to house asian families on the estate. When the tenants refused to give the Commission an undertaking not to apply further pressure to the landlord, the case was taken to court. Subsequently, the tenants gave an undertaking to the court that they would not further breach section 31 of the Race Relations Act 1976. This undertaking could be enforced like any injunction.

CHAPTER 6

PREVENTATIVE ACTION

Introduction

Notwithstanding the suggestions in the previous chapter, the law offers only limited and lengthy redress for people being racially harassed. If the landlord seeks and obtains a possession order, the case could last for several months. The person being harassed will receive no compensation for the distress which they may have suffered, and indeed they may attract further hostility.

Whilst it is important that landlords show their commitment to implementing their racial harassment policy by taking legal action where appropriate when cases have arisen, and by making it known they are not afraid to take such action, a racial harassment policy should also include action to reduce the likelihood of harassment occurring in the first place.

Just as dealing with racial harassment when it has occurred involves responses by several agencies, so does preventative action. The roles which some agencies might play are set out below.

Tenants' and residents' associations

Tenants' associations and residents' associations have a potentially valuable role in preventing racial harassment. Some landlords include specific references to the role of tenants' associations in their racial harassment policies. The London Borough of Hounslow, for example, states in its racial harassment policy:

> It is the aim of a well organised, active and committed tenants' association that the welfare and interest of their members are upheld and represented – both for harmony and good neighbour relations and that all unsocial activities are stamped out. People being racially harassed should be offered support from their local tenants' association in time of their greatest need for help. Tenants' associations needing assistance and guidance should be offered help from their area tenant support and race support worker to deal with racism on the estate.

Leicester City Council recommends that:

> The area office staff will encourage tenants' associations to adopt an active role in welcoming new tenants to their estates, and introducing them to neighbours, local amenities and organisations. The area office staff should also provide information and assistance to tenants' associations in order that they may promote anti-racist work and policies. During attendance at tenants' association meetings staff will encourage and monitor the tenants' association's compliance with the council's equal opportunities policy, and advise the tenants' associ-

ation on the provision of activities designed to reflect racial composition of the area. Staff will also assist with the development within tenants' associations of their own Equal Opportunities Policy including the positive recruiting of black tenants.

Some housing associations too are now seeking to involve tenants' associations in dealing with racial harassment. One example of this is the Liverpool Housing Trust which is developing a joint approach to combatting racial harassment with its Runcorn residents' associations.

Landlords should ensure that tenants' or residents' associations in their area are made aware of their policies. Table 7 below sets out steps for encouraging tenants' associations to become involved in preventative action.

Table 7 Tenants' association involvement: key points

1 Set out in racial harassment policies and guidance the ways in which tenants' associations, tenants' federations or other tenants' consultative groups are expected to assist landlords.

2 Explain the need for a racial harassment policy to tenants' associations and welcoming their comments when consulting tenants over including a 'no harassment' clause in the tenancy agreement (see Tables 8 and 9).

3 Encourage tenants' associations to take steps to prevent racial harassment on their estates.

4 Encourage tenants' associations to support victims of racial harassment, always bearing in mind the wishes of the person being harassed, and their right to privacy.

5 Encourage tenants' associations to assist in the identification of perpetrators of racial harassment.

6 Monitor racial harassment with tenants' associations at relevant consultative bodies such as area committees or neighbourhood forums.

Other policies

As noted in Chapter 4, account should be taken of the relationship between the allocations policy and the racial harassment policy – including how to allocate where there has been harassment, and ways of ensuring that individuals and families are not left isolated and vulnerable to harassment.

Housing staff

Housing staff, including estate officers, caretakers, wardens, maintenance officers, have an important role in preventing harassment, by:

— providing support for potentially vulnerable tenants

— identifying incidents at the earliest opportunity

— actively discouraging racist behaviour among other tenants.

Other agencies

Landlords should liaise with other agencies such as the police, schools, youth clubs and community groups to build up information-gathering networks to aid prevention and early identification of incidents. Agencies working together can help spot any trends of harassment, for example, the same offenders, the same people being harassed, the same type or time of incidents (see also Chapter 8).

'No harassment' clause in tenancy

The importance of having a 'no harassment' clause in the tenancy agreement was noted in Chapter 5. This clause should be explained to all new tenants at signing-up, explaining the kind of behaviour that might constitute 'nuisance and annoyance'; that 'neighbours' includes anyone who is affected, not just immediate neighbours; and also that tenants are responsible for any nuisance caused by their children and visitors. Tables 8 and 9 below set out the terms of a model 'no harassment' clause.

If a landlord decides to add a specific harassment clause to the tenancy agreement, there will need to be consultation on this. This should be carefully handled. In order to avoid misunderstanding, it is good practice to hold meetings with tenants to explain the purpose of the clause – to deter harassers and to reassure people who might experience harassment – before the formal letter of consultation is sent. Without an adequate preliminary explanation, there is a risk that people who receive the letter will feel that they are being accused of harassment.

Some tenants may want the clause better explained; others may have different views about how to tackle harassment. Some may object to the clause altogether. All these matters can be discussed at the meeting. It should be stressed that the landlord's obligation is limited to consulting the tenants. The tenants do not have the right to veto any changes in the terms of the tenancy. It is hard to imagine what legitimate grounds a tenant could have for objecting to this clause as, if they are not perpetrators of harassment it will not affect them, and many other social landlords already have it.

Once views of tenants have been collected, the tenancy agreement can be altered.

Table 8 Model 'no harassment' clause in local authority tenancy agreements

1 The tenant shall act in a reasonable manner and must not do anything which causes nuisance, annoyance or offence to other tenants or their family, lodgers or visitors, or damage to any property or possessions belonging to the landlord, or to its tenants, their family, lodgers or visitors or to the tenant's neighbours.

2 Without prejudice to the generality of the above, the clause applies to acts of discrimination, intimidation or harassment on any of the following grounds: race, nationality, sex, sexual orientation, religious or political beliefs, age or disability.

3 The tenant will be responsible for the conduct of all members of the tenant's family and other residents at or visitors to the premises.

4 Breach of this clause will normally lead to eviction proceedings, in which the tenant may not be eligible for rehousing.

(*A local authority could add:*)

5 In line with its commitment to an equal opportunities policy and in compliance with its duty under section 71 of the Race Relations Act 1976 to eliminate unlawful racial discrimination, the council will always evict tenants who have been in breach of this provision where a court order has been obtained.

Table 9 Model 'no harassment' clause in housing association tenancy agreements

(*The National Federation of Housing Associations suggests the following wording which may be used in both secure and assured tenancy agreements:*)

Racial and other harassment – the tenant's obligations: not to commit or allow members of his/her household or invited visitors to commit any form of harassment on the grounds of race, colour, religion, sex, sexual orientation or disability which may interfere with the peace and comfort of, or cause offence to, any other tenant, member of his/her household, visitors or neighbours.

CHAPTER 7

PUBLICISING THE POLICY AND RAISING AWARENESS

One of the most important ways a landlord has of preventing racial harassment is to publicise and raise awareness about its policy. This has a two-fold effect. It demonstrates to people who are being harassed, or fear it, that their landlord will provide them with support and assistance. It also warns putative perpetrators of the action their landlord will take against them, including eviction.

Publicity methods

Landlords may publicise their racial harassment policies in a number of formal and informal ways which include:

— when new tenants sign their tenancy agreement

— by articles in newsletters and annual reports

— press publicity when successful legal action has been taken against a perpetrator

— by councillors, committee members and staff challenging racist comments at meetings

— by leaflets, videos and posters displayed at the landlords' own premises and those used by local organisations such as community groups, schools, youth clubs, race equality councils, citizens' advice bureaux, law centres and referral agencies.

As noted above, residents' and tenants' associations can be an excellent way of helping a message travel by word of mouth. Community and estate workers are another good local source to reinforce the message. As is stressed in Chapter 9, this can be done most accurately and effectively if all frontline staff receive training on the procedures and policy.

The message

Publicity material should include a clear statement of commitment. The Lambeth Housing Services's statement of intent reads as follows:

> Lambeth Council condemns all forms of racial discrimination and strongly believes in racial equality. It will take whatever steps it can to stamp out all forms of racial discrimination and harassment and to ensure that everyone can live anywhere in Lambeth free from intimidation and abuse.

It is best not to put too many details of the policy in leaflets but to stress that action will be taken against offenders and support and confidentiality is offered to people being harassed. The Guinness Trust's leaflet, for example, states:

Help and support will be offered by staff to people being harassed. Firm action will be taken against those involved in harassment, ranging from written warnings to legal action for possession of the home of a tenant found responsible for harassment. The tenancy agreements clearly state that tenants are responsible for the actions of all members of their households and any visitors to their home.

CHAPTER 8

ADMINISTRATIVE PROCEDURES

Introduction

Much time and effort goes into drawing up a racial harassment policy. It is therefore important that a landlord expends similar effort in developing the necessary administrative procedures in order that the policy is effectively put into practice.

The administrative procedures must be able to respond quickly and efficiently to an incident of racial harassment. Action may, for example, need to be taken to secure a property so that a tenant can continue to live there in safety. The procedures should also be designed to enable information to be collected accurately, bearing in mind that evidence may be required for a later court case.

Racial harassment administrative procedures should enable a landlord both to take appropriate action in an individual case and allow monitoring of a number of cases to identify any patterns of harassment. There should be some way of collating cases reported to the landlord. Where possible, local agencies should collectively review their response to racial harassment in order to develop more effective, co-ordinated action.

It is also important that procedures serve the objective of stopping the harassment, and do not, as is a danger with following any procedure, become an end in itself.

Using existing procedures

Landlords will probably be able to use some of their existing administrative procedures to tackle racial harassment. Most landlords have developed systems for responding to repairs, for example. These typically state that emergency repairs must be completed within 12 and 24 hours.

Such a repairs procedure could form part of a landlord's response to racial harassment. Landlords should check that their emergency repairs schedules cover all possible repairs arising from an incident of racial harassment. Removing graffiti is not always included. Where this is not the case, the emergency repairs procedure should be amended to ensure that racist graffiti will be removed within 24 hours (see also Chapter 4).

Record keeping

An incident of racial harassment may be reported to a landlord through a variety of channels (see Chapter 3). All incidents should be directed to the designated investigating officer as quickly as possible. One way of doing this is by using a racial harassment initial report form, an example of which is shown in Appendix 2. This should enable whoever is first notified of an incident to record basic details, and include the following information:

— Name of person reporting incident

— Name of person experiencing harassment, if different

— Name of tenant, if different

— Ethnic origin of person experiencing harassment

— Is an interpreter needed? Which language?

— Nature of incident

— Time and place

— Investigating officer.

If a landlord uses this approach, it is a good practice to ensure that all of the channels through which an incident might be reported have copies of the form.

It is also good practice for the investigating officer to be responsible for opening an individual file on the case and for logging the incident in the landlord's central racial harassment file and the tenancy files. The central racial harassment file should be kept by the landlord's racial harassment co-ordinator, who needs to be a suitably placed member of staff, such as a senior manager or a race and housing officer.

Investigating officers should use a report form to assist carrying out their initial interview with the person being harassed, observing the guidelines for interviews set out in the policy. An example is given in

Appendix 3. This form should enable the investigating officer to gain a detailed picture of the incident, a description of the perpetrators if known, whether there were any witnesses and if the police have been involved. The form should also allow space for the investigating officer to record what action has been taken to date so the person being harassed can be kept informed and a record made of further action proposed in the light of the initial investigation. So, the form should include:

— Date and time of incident

— Details of incident, eg, verbal abuse, graffiti

— Description of people carrying out the harassment, eg, number of people, ages, clothes, height, race

— Action taken by tenant, eg, called police, notified caretaker

— Action taken by others, eg, police, tenants' association

— Details of any witnesses who might have seen or heard incident.

Landlords may find it useful to devise a diary of incidents. This form should be left by the investigating officer with the people being harassed so they can record any further incidents of racial harassment. Information of this kind could be very important in later action against perpetrators. An example is given in Appendix 7.

It is good practice to include a mechanism to review progress in dealing with an incident of racial harassment. This can be done by using panels or working parties for monitoring (see Appendix 12). Progress should be reviewed at regular intervals, not just shortly after an incident first occurred. For example, a decision may have been taken to transfer the person being harassed. It is not always possible to do this immediately, so, to minimise delay, the case should be reviewed every four to six weeks.

Guide letters

Landlords may find it useful to have guide letters to send to alleged perpetrators and to the police. Examples of these are given in Appendix 8 and 9. One standard letter should be of a general nature, addressed to residents in a block or on an estate, where it has not be possible to identify precisely who are the perpetrators. Landlords may also find it useful to have standard letters to the local police. The letter should request that the police assists the landlord in investigating an incident of racial harassment.

It is not appropriate to use standard formats for letters to individual perpetrators.

Information storage

Copies of all the above forms should be retained on the tenancy file of the person being harassed. Where the matter goes beyond one incident, a case file should be established within the tenancy files of the person being harassed so that progress on an individual case can be easily monitored. In addition, for monitoring purposes, a central racial harassment file will be needed, containing all of the above forms, together with any correspondence either with those experiencing the harassment, with actual or suspected perpetrators, or with other agencies such as the police. Correspondence with perpetrators, together with notes of any interviews, or letters to other agencies about the perpetrator should also be kept on the tenancy file of the perpetrator.

Monitoring further action

Landlords should not only monitor progress in dealing with individual incidents of racial harassment. They should also have administrative procedures for monitoring the overall picture of racial harassment in their area of operation.

One way of doing this is by convening regular meetings of representatives from the different bodies which, together with the landlord, have developed the multi-agency approach discussed in Chapter 4. Such meetings should be held at least four times a year. Multi-agency meetings can be used to review progress and develop further action to tackle racial harassment on a number of fronts as set out in Table 10 below.

Table 10 Multi-agency action: key points

1 Crime prevention measures to increase personal safety or security on an estate
2 Joint action for dealing with individual cases
3 Joint action in developing working relationships for dealing with future cases

---

4 Joint publicity about consequences for perpetrators of harassment

5 Information sharing to draw up a complete picture of the level of the problem in a particular area

6 Information transfer where an agency is aware that it is not the appropriate one to deal with certain types of cases to another agency which is better placed (see also below)

7 Putting together as much evidence as possible about a particular case

8 Support for the person being harassed by co-ordinating the agencies involved so that their actions are complementary and not contradictory.

It is good practice to develop, where possible, joint administrative procedures to enable multi-agency meetings to review progress and develop further action to tackle racial harassment. It is most important that the agencies involved agree a common definition of racial harassment. Where possible, they should also use common forms and administrative procedures, or at least forms which use the same core elements so that information can be easily shared and collated.

Another alternative is a racial harassment working party. Suggested terms of reference are given in Appendix 12.

Confidentiality

It is essential that landlords ensure that confidentiality is maintained throughout their procedures for dealing with incidents of racial harassment. Racial harassment files should be stored in a secure place with access limited to those officers directly involved in a case. Any public reports prepared should be written in such as way as to ensure that no person being harassed can be identified from them. Investigating officers should ensure that they have the written consent of people being harassed before they divulge information about the case to an outside agency.

Procedures flow chart

Set out below is a flow chart summarising the key stages in the administrative procedures designed to deal quickly and effectively with incidents of racial harassment.

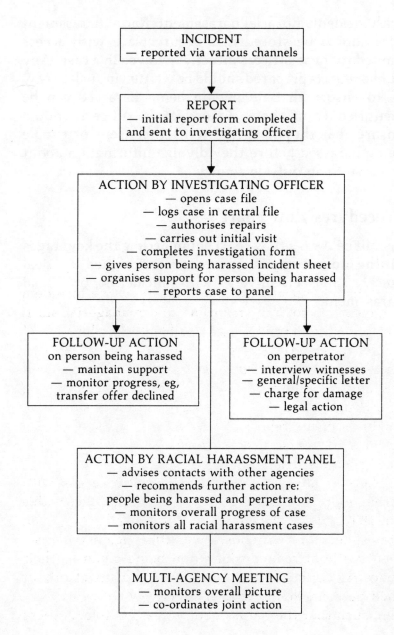

CHAPTER 9

TRAINING OF STAFF

Role of training

An effective racial harassment strategy will include a commitment to train frontline and managerial staff. The role of such training is to enable the landlord's staff to recognise and deal effectively with incidents of racial harassment, in accordance with the organisation's policy and procedures. Training should include both knowledge-based awareness training for all staff who might receive a report of harassment and skills-based training for housing management staff. Managers too need specialist training.

There is always a danger in sensitive areas with strong moral imperatives to 'do something' such as this one that staff will be enjoined to effort and action in an atmosphere of righteous indignation against harassment without real consideration being given to their concerns, doubts, lack of confidence and anxiety about their personal ability to deal effectively with the problem, such that the harassment will stop. Indeed, there have been examples in housing organisations of such a febrile atmosphere having been generated that the mere expression of doubt is taken as evidence of lack of commitment to solving the problem. Training sessions, which have clear ground rules of confidentiality and respect, are the appropriate place for these concerns to be aired, for confidence to be built, and for doubts to be resolved jointly.

The CRE cited the following examples of good practice in its investigation into housing associations:

> One association used training videos as part of their sessions to provide staff with some background into the general problems of racial harassment. This was coupled with relevant staff spending a day with senior officers responsible for investigating incidents for them to gain an insight into the practical handling of cases. At least one association made racial harassment training mandatory for all frontline staff such as receptionists and also other junior staff such as wardens and maintenance workers who had regular contact with tenants.

Aims and objectives

Like any training course, racial harassment training should have clear aims and objectives. These will help focus the training and provide a way for the landlord to evaluate the effectiveness of the training. The precise aims and objectives of a racial harassment training course will vary according to the needs of the landlord and the participants attending the training. Examples of approaches to training are given in Appendix 10 and 11.

The overall aim of each course should be to assist the participants to implement the organisation's racial harassment policies and procedures. In order to fulfil this overall aim, a racial harassment course could have the following, more specific objectives:

— understanding the organisation's definition of racial harassment, centred on the person being harassed

— being able to identify and respond to incidents of racial harassment in line with their role in the organisation's policy and procedures

— understanding what steps they and the organisation can take to prevent harassment

— knowing how to interview people being harassed and alleged perpetrators of racial harassment, if that is part of their job responsibilities

— being aware of the need to co-operate with other agencies, and the mechanisms for doing so, in order to tackle racial harassment.

Key issues

Some examples of the issues to cover on a racial harassment training course include: the background to racial harassment (both national and local); the landlord's commitment to tackle racial harassment; the landlord's definition of racial harassment; key aspects of the landlord's racial harassment policy and procedures such as:

— immediate action to support people being harassed, including repairs

— responding to 'out-of-hours' incidents

— conducting interviews with people being harassed and perpetrators

— collecting evidence

— taking action within set down time limits

— monitoring progress on individual cases

— links with outside bodies such as the police, voluntary agencies, education and social services departments

— the support staff require to put the policy and procedures into practice

— monitoring the overall effectiveness of the policy and procedures.

The precise set of issues to cover on a racial harassment course will again vary according to the needs of the landlord and participants. A course for senior staff would focus on their role in ensuring the racial harassment policy and procedures are being put into practice, and regularly reviewed, while a course for frontline staff would focus on how to provide an immediate, effective response to an incident.

Participants

Training should be arranged for all those involved in putting a landlord's racial harassment policy and procedures into practice. This means that the participants should include:

— estate management staff, both junior and senior

— caretakers and other scheme based staff such as wardens

— reception staff

— repairs and maintenance staff

— race and housing officers.

Where possible, training should be extended beyond the landlord's staff. Tenants' and residents' associations and other voluntary groups which have a part to play in implementing a racial harassment strategy should also receive training. This should concentrate on matters like providing support for people being harassed, isolating perpetrators and taking steps to prevent racial harassment occurring in the first place.

Delivery of training

Racial harassment training can be carried out by internal trainers, external trainers or a combination of the two. Possible internal trainers include race and housing officers, a landlord's generic training officer and line managers. The London Borough of Ealing, for example, have run a training for trainers course for line managers specifically designed to equip them to run racial harassment training courses for their junior staff. Possible external trainers include consultants who specialise in racial harassment training or representatives of local community organisations.

The pros and cons of each option are discussed more fully in the CRE's *Training for Racial Equality* (1989). For example, race and housing officers or community organisations should know about local incidents of racial harassment but they may lack training expertise. Conversely, consultants should be good trainers but may lack local knowledge. A landlord must therefore be clear about the aims and objectives of the racial harassment training and that whoever runs the training can devise and run an appropriate course.

CHAPTER 10

REVIEWING POLICIES AND PROCEDURES

It is vitally important to review policies and procedures for stopping racial harassment regularly, at least every three years. The first stage in reviewing policies and procedures is to review the use that has been made of the policy.

Reporting of cases

The first question should be how many cases have been reported? The CRE found in its investigation *Housing Associations and Racial Equality in Scotland* (1993), in common with previous studies already cited in Chapter 1, that while many associations had policies, in many cases they had been used infrequently or not at all. This should not, however, be taken as evidence that there is no problem with racial harassment in the area. The evidence shown in Chapter 1 indicates that it is a national problem. A more likely explanation is that those experiencing harassment know nothing of the organisation's policies, or, if they do, they have little confidence either in the seriousness of the landlord's intentions, or in their ability to actually do anything to stop the harassment. There could hardly be a more compelling case for reviewing policies, particularly those parts dealing with publicity and raising awareness of policies (see Chapter 7).

Effectiveness of policy

There are three other areas that should be the subject of inquiry when reviewing policies and procedures:

— has the policy been followed when complaints have been made?

— has the outcome of the case been satisfactory, both from the point of view of the landlord, and the complainant?

— was the speed with which cases have been dealt been satisfactory?

Review process

In order to establish the answer to these questions, and the previously mentioned areas of concern about awareness of, and confidence in the policy, a senior member of housing management staff should be given responsibility for consulting with complainants and staff who have used the policies and procedures to ascertain their views about whether existing arrangements are satisfactory and, if not, how they could be improved.

It is important to stress the need for 'user', or tenant

involvement. This is the only sure way of guaranteeing that policies focus on the outcomes desired by those experiencing harassment, and that procedures do not become a bureaucratic labrynth, designed to give the impression of much effort, without much regard for the effectiveness of the result. Once these views have been garnered, policies and procedures can be re-drafted in the light of them.

When new policies and procedures have been drafted previous complainants and affected staff should once more be asked their views, with a deadline given for the receipt of responses. After final versions have been drafted, taking comments into account where appropriate, they should be launched both in writing, and at verbal briefing sessions by line managers responsible for staff who will be implementing the new policies and procedures. Staff members should be given the opportunity to share concerns and to resolve dilemmas and problems together.

There may in addition be a need for a revised training programme (see Chapter 9) to take into account changed policy objectives, new procedures, and the ever-present requirement for the deepening and extension of the skills base of housing management staff in this difficult area.

APPENDICES

APPENDICES

Appendix 1
Suggested policy statement on harassment in housing

Definition

Harassment is deliberate violence which may be verbal or physical, and which includes attacks on property as well as on the person. The motivation for harassment may include race, religion, colour, ethnic origin, gender, sexuality and disability, amongst others. In many cases the person experiencing the harassment will know the motive of the perpetrator. Their perception of the motive should be the basis for taking appropriate action to stop the harassment. In others, there will be evidence of the motive, such as graffiti or language.

Our policy

We deplore harassment. In dealing with harassment in our housing we will seek to:

1 **Stop the harassment**
2 **Support the person being harassed**
3 **Take action against perpetrators.**

The way we deal with harassment

Step 1 The report of the incident of harassment will be recorded by which ever member of staff receives it. This will not necessarily be some-one in housing management. It may be a receptionist or a member of maintenance staff.

Step 2   Immediate maintenance work will be undertaken as necessary, for example, removing graffiti, repairing windows, improving the security of property. This should be treated as emergency work and therefore completed within 48 hours, at the most.

Step 3   Housing management staff will interview the person who has been harassed as soon as possible, definitely within 24 hours.

The details of the incident, including dates, times and witnesses will be recorded. The notes will be agreed with the person who has experienced the harassment.

If a crime has been committed and the tenant wishes to involve the police, they will be contacted immediately. Delay may prejudice the outcome of any criminal proceedings.

The organisations's policy and procedure will be explained to the tenant who has been harassed.

Options for action can then be discussed, including visiting and warning the perpetrator and ways of increasing support to the tenant.

Supporting the person who has been harassed and acting against the perpetrator are not seen as alternatives. They should be acted on concurrently.

We recognise that it may take several visits to the tenant who has been harassed before they have sufficient confidence in the organisation and trust in the individual housing manager to consent to a visit being made to the perpetrator.

A course of action can then be agreed, summarised and noted. Some measures to support those who have been harassed may involve other agencies such as helplines, law centres, victim support schemes, and the police.

Forms for the recording of any further incidents will be shown and explained to the tenant. They are available in the appropriate languages. The forms will then be left with the tenants for them to complete.

Interviewers will stress the need to report immediately any further incidents.

Step 4 If the tenant who experienced the harassment has consented, the perpetrator may then be interviewed by housing management staff.

Step 5 A follow-up letter will be sent to the perpetrator confirming the discussion that took place, re-stating relevant clauses in the tenancy agreement and the organisation's objectives to stop harassment, support the person being harassed and take action against perpetrators.

Step 6   The person who has been harassed will be kept informed of action taken and visited regularly, at least once a week, to ensure that harassment has not re-started and not been reported. Where regular visits are not possible frequent contact by telephone will be maintained. Wardens, caretakers and any other estate-based staff will, with the consent of the person who has been harassed, be briefed on incidents and any action taken so that they can offer continuous support to the anyone who is being harassed.

Step 7   Further incidents of harassment might lead to more severe warnings being given to the perpetrator and ultimately, criminal proceedings, injunctions or possession proceedings under the tenancy agreement.

Each visit to the perpetrator should be followed up by a letter recording the discussion, and noting any action that the organisation might take.

Step 8   Increased support can be provided to the person experiencing the harassment as necessary. In some cases this may include moving them to another property. Whilst this is not desirable as it means that they suffer the loss of their home and no action is take against the perpetrator, it may be the only way for them to feel secure. Where this is necessary, it will be done as quickly as possible. Some indication of how long it will take to arrange a suitable move will be given to the tenant. Care will be taken to ensure that the property they move to is of no worse quality than the one they are leaving. In some cases the move will be temporary while action is taken to stop the harassment.

Step 9 Repeated visits to the perpetrator will be made if harassment persists or recurs after a break.

Step 10 Legal action against perpetrators will be taken if warnings fail.

Step 11 All incidents are recorded and monitored centrally, not just on tenants' files, and are treated confidentially. Regular reports on themes and issues, as well as overview statistics are regularly presented to the racial harassment working party, at least annually.

Step 12 The effectiveness of this policy is reviewed at least every three years, and more often when necessary.

Appendix 2

Form A
Initial report form
(To be filled in by whoever receives the complaint)

Confidential: racial harassment

1   Name of person experiencing harassment........

2   Address...

3   Telephone number ....

4   Ethnic origin *(NB These are the categories recommended by the CRE. They may need amending in the light of local circumstances.)*

    (a)   Black/White.
    (b)   African/Caribbean/Indian/Pakistani/
        Bangladeshi/Irish/Chinese/British.
    (c)   Other (please specify).

5   Is the person experiencing harassment our tenant? Yes/No

6   If no, what is their relationship to any of our tenants?...

7   Description of the incident

    (a)   What happened?...............................
        ....
    (b)   When did it happen (date and time)?.........
    (c)   Where exactly did it happen? ....
        ....

(d) Are any repairs needed? ....

8   Who is this report to be passed to?...................

9   Name of person who took the report...............

10 Date...

(Copies to: tenant's file and racial harassment file)

Appendix 3

Form B
Report of visit to person experiencing harassment
(To be filled in by investigating officer either at the interview, or immediately upon return to the office)

Confidential: racial harassment

1   Personal details

    (a)   Name of tenant or person affected............

    (b)   Address......................................

    (c)   Ethnic origin
        — Black/White.
        — African/Caribbean/Indian/Pakistani/
           Bangladeshi/Irish/Chinese/British.
        — Other (please specify).

2   First language ....

3   Interpreter needed? Yes/No

4   Details of visit
    (a)   Date of visit................................
    (b)   Name(s) of visiting officer(s)......................

5   Description of incident

    (a)   What happened?..............................

    ....

    (b)   When did it happen (date and time)?.........
    (c)   Where exactly did it happen? ....

6 Witnesses

   (a) Did anyone see the incident happen? Yes/ No

   (b) If yes, does the tenant know their name(s) or their address(es)?.................................

7 Personal injury

   — Was the complainant hurt? Briefly describe the injury ....

       ....

8 Damage to property

   — Was there any damage to the property? ...

   (NB Take photographs of damage to property for file)

9 Perpetrator

   (a) Does the tenant know who attacked them or their home? Yes/No

   (b) Was there more than one person involved? Yes/No

   (c) If the tenant does know who they are, what did the tenant think their ethnic origin was?...

   (d) If the tenant does know them, do they know their name(s) or address(es)? ....

   (f) Would the tenant be willing to allow you to visit the perpetrator(s) so long as you respected their confidentiality? Yes/No

8 Involvement of police

   (a) Has the tenant informed the police? Yes/No

   (b) If yes, what was their response?...............

       ....

(c) If no, do they want the police informed?
Yes/No

(d) If the tenant would like the name of the
police officer or department who deals
specifically with racial attacks, note contact
name and phone number............................

9   Involvement of other support agencies

(a) Has the tenant contacted any other agencies? Yes/No

(b) If yes, which ones? Note their name,
address, phone number and the name of the
person contacted..

(c) Does the tenant need the names, addresses
and phone numbers of any other local
support agency? Note those given.............
....

10 Support for the tenant

(a) Does the tenant need any other help, such
as telephones, personal alarms, transfer
application form, temporary accommodation? Yes/No

(b) If yes, what help does the tenant need?.....
....

11 Attacks on other people

—   Does the tenant know if there have been
similar attacks on other people in the neighbourhood? Note names and addresses.......

12 Signature of interviewer...................................

13 Date and time of completing form....................

14 Has this form been read, or read to, and under-
    stood by the tenant? Yes/No
    (Copies to: new case file; tenant's file; racial harassment file)

Appendix 4

Form C
Prompt for visit to suspected perpetrator
(To be completed in advance by the two interviewers and to be taken to the interview. Both interviewers should have a copy)

Confidential: racial harassment

1 Name of investigating officer...............................

2 Name of accompanying officer...........................

3 Date form completed..

4 Checklist

— Three copies of the following documents are needed – for both interviewers and one to be left with the perpetrator: relevant clause in tenancy agreement/racial harassment policy/racial harassment procedure.

5 Interview

(a) Introductions ....

(b) Reason for visit ....

(c) Descriptions of the incidents that have been reported

....

....

(d) Summary of clause in tenancy agreement

....

(e) Summary of landlord's policy and procedure..

....

(f) Summary of what action the landlord might take..
....

(g) At the end of the interview how are you going to communicate to each other that you think the interview should be terminated?..

(h) What are you going to say to end the interview?..
....

(Copies to: suspected perpetrator's file/case file/file of tenant being harassed/racial harassment file)

Appendix 5

Form D
Record of responses from suspected perpetrator
(These should be recorded by the person accompanying the investigating officer. The notes should reflect as exactly as possible what the perpetrator says, not judgements made by the person taking the notes. Agreed questions can be entered on the form in advance)

Confidential: racial harassment

1   Name of investigating officer..............................

2   Name of accompanying officer.........................

3   Date form completed................................

4   Perpetrator's responses in detail

    — immediate response to visit and your description of incidents..............................
....

5   Answers to specific questions

    — question 1...
    answer...
    — question 2...
    answer...
    — question 3...
    answer...
    — question 4...
    answer...

— question 5..

answer..

— question 6..

answer..

5 Any other responses?...

6 Date and time when notes made.......................

7 Place where notes made....................................

8 Name of notetaker ....

9 Job title...

10 Signature...

(Copies to suspected perpetrator's file/case file/file of tenant being harassed/racial harassment file)

Appendix 6

Form E
Follow-up action
(To be completed by housing officer)

Confidential: racial harassment

1 Name of housing officer...................................

2 Date form completed...

3 Has the perpetrator been written to summarising the discussion and re-stating any agreed next steps? Yes/No

4 Date of letter..

5 Have copies of the letter gone to the case file, the suspected perpetrator's file, the file of the tenant being harassed and the central racial harassment file? Yes/No

6 Have the necessary monitoring forms been filled in and circulated? Yes/No

7 Has the case been discussed with your line manager? Yes/No

8 What further action is needed?........................
....

9 Which other agencies need to be informed?.....
....

10 Dates they are to be/have been informed.........

11 Have copies of letter(s) to other agencies or notes of meetings gone to the case file, the file of the person being harassed and the perpetrator's file, and the central racial harassment file? Yes/ No

12 What feedback is to be given to the tenant being harassed? ....

13 What measures need to be taken to protect the tenant from any reprisals? ....

Appendix 7

Form F
Diary of incidents
(Make four extra copies of the incident record part of this form for the complainant's use)

Confidential: racial harassment

In order to support you and, if appropriate, take action against the people who are attacking you, we need as much information as possible. It would help us if you would keep a note of any further incidents on this sheet. It would also help if you would record all incidents whether they happen in your home or somewhere else.

The following information would be particularly helpful:
the identity or description of the people who harass you; anyone else who sees or hears the incident; any contact with the police, that is the name, rank, number and station of any officers you have spoken to.

If more than five incidents occur, please contact your housing officer. The housing officer will come and see you to find out details about what has been happening, and to give you more forms on which to record what has been going on.

Name of complainant ....

Name of tenant, if different....................................

Address...

Telephone number...

1   Description of incident

   (a)   What happened?...

   (b)   When did it happen (date and time)?.........

   (c)   Where did it happen?................................

2   Did anyone else see the incident happen? Yes/
   No

   —   if yes, do you know their name(s) or their
      address(es)?..

3   Were you, or anyone else who with you, hurt?
   Briefly describe ....

4   Describe any damage to your property?...........

   ....

5   Do you know who attacked you or your home?
   Yes/No

6   Was there more than one person involved? Yes/
   No

7   If you do know who they are, what did you think
   their ethnic origin was? ....

8   If you do know them, do you know their name(s)
   or address(es)?..

9   Did you inform the police? Yes/No

10   If yes, what was their response?......................

Appendix 8

Guide letter to tenants
(General letter to all tenants who may be involved)

Dear tenant

I am writing to inform you, and all our other tenants in the area, about an incident that recently took place in your neighbourhood. *(Describe the nature of the incident. Do not give the identity of the person who was attacked or harassed. Do not be too specific about times and places.)*

As landlord we want to make it clear to all our tenants that we take these incidents extremely seriously. The tenancy agreement states that we will seek possession of the home of any of our tenants who harass their neighbours. It also states that tenants are responsible for the behaviour of everyone who lives in or visits their home. A copy of the relevant clause of your tenancy agreement is enclosed.

Our policy is to investigate all incidents of this kind, and, where appropriate, take action against those who do them. We will also involve the police if necessary.

If you have any information about these or other similar incidents please contact *(give name and phone number of housing officer)*. All information will be treated confidentially.

We are sure that most of our tenants are as keen as we are to stop harassment or nuisance to other tenants, and so we would be grateful for your co-operation.

Yours faithfully

Appendix 9

Guide letter to police

Dear Chief Superintendent

We are the landlords of *(give address)*. We have recently had reported to us some incidents about which we are very concerned *(give dates and describe incidents – only give name and address of the tenant being harassed with their consent)*.

You will understand that we want to protect our tenants from this kind of behaviour and we will do everything in our power as landlords to stop it. We do, however, need the support of the police, both to deter perpetrators and stop the behaviour, and also, where appropriate to take action against the perpetrators.

I would be grateful if one of your officers could contact me as soon as possible to discuss this case.

Yours sincerely

Appendix 10

Training programme on dealing with racial harassment

Objectives

By the end of the course participants should:

— understand the organisation's definition of racial harassment, centred on the person being harassed

— be able to identify and respond to incidents of racial harassment in line with the organisation's policy and procedures

— know how to interview people being harassed and alleged perpetrators of racial harassment

— be aware of the need to co-operate with other agencies to tackle racial harassment

Programme

DAY ONE

09.30   Welcome and introductions
Course aim and objectives

09.50   Stereotyping, prejudice and discrimination
Small group exercise and video extract

10.30   Racial harassment policy
Background
Definition of racial harassment

11.00   Break

11.15   Racial harassment: the role of the police
        Video extract followed by a question and
        answer session introduced by Inspector Jones,
        Community Liaison Officer

12.15   Lunch

13.15   Racial harassment policy
        Introduction to the procedures followed by
        case studies covering individual incidents
        Presentations and discussion

14.45   Break

15.00   Landlord's racial harassment policy
        Case studies on involving other agencies
        Presentations and discussion

16.30   Close

DAY TWO

09.30   Interview skills
        The importance of listening
        Preparing for and conducting interviews
        Video extract

10.45   Break

11.00   Racial harassment interviews
        Interviewing people being harassed
        Interviewing alleged perpetrators of racial
        harassment

12.30   Lunch

13.30   Putting the skills into practice
        A series of exercises designed to give course

members the chance to put their interview skills and knowledge of the racial harassment procedures into practice

15.00   Break

15.15   Exercises continued

16.00   Recap and final remarks

16.30   Close

Appendix 11

Modular approach to training in dealing with racial harassment

An alternative approach to racial harassment training is to run a series of training modules covering different aspects of a landlord's policies and procedures. These modules could comprise:

Module 1 – Introduction, policy and procedure (one day)

Objectives

1   To define what constitutes racial harassment as distinct from neighbour disputes or rowdy behaviour. To consider what forms it can take.

2   To examine the social context in which racial harassment occurs and the reasons why incidents are unacknowledged and unreported.

3   To identify ways of ensuring that incidents of racial harassment come to the notice of the landlord's staff and are properly recorded.

4   To define what is meant by a 'victim-centred' approach in dealing with racial harassment.

5   To familiarise staff with the landlord's policies for dealing with racial harassment.

6   To ensure that staff are familiar with the administrative and procedural framework for reporting, recording and acting on incidents of racial harassment.

7   To identify and confirm the roles of different members of staff in dealing with racial harassment.

Module 2 – Supporting, negotiating, mediating (one day)

Objectives

1   To identify the types of support needed by victims of racial harassment.

2   To identify ways of dealing with perpetrators of racial harassment, persuasive and statutory, both tenants of the landlord and others.

3   To identify the inter-personal skills necessary for staff to be able to handle conflict between victims and perpetrators.

4   To give participants an opportunity to practice and develop these skills through case studies and role play.

5   To identify which other agencies to liaise with and when, including the police, solicitors, victim support organisations.

Module 3 – Sanctions and legal remedies (one day)

Objectives

1   To identify legal remedies available for dealing with the perpetrators including:

   — injunctions to secure an end to harassment

— criminal damage
— assault
— public order offences
— possession proceedings.

2   To ensure that participants understand and can use legal methods of taking notes and keeping records, taking statements from witnesses etc., which could be used in legal proceedings.

Module 4 – Managing action on racial harassment (half day)

Objectives

1   To identify effective approaches and methods for managers to monitor and review the handling of incidents of racial harassment by staff.

2   To establish and review effective methods of reporting to committees incidents of racial harassment and responses to them.

3   To identify managers' responsibility for briefing and training new members of staff.

Appendix 12

Suggested terms of reference for racial harassment working parties or panels

Membership...

Convenor/Secretary..

Chair...

Circulation list for minutes..

The role of the working party

1 To receive regular reports from the director of housing and director of the legal department, or solicitors, relating to current individual racial harassment cases or cases handled since the last working party meeting.

2 To review and monitor:

   (a) the decision of the district housing manager as to the level of sanction appropriate.

   (b) the advice of the legal department or solicitors.

   (c) the implementation of any decision made by the district housing manager or other delegated housing officer.

   (d) the progress of any court action.

3 To make recommendations to the district housing manager of alternative strategies for particular cases, as appropriate, including remedies that the legal department, or the landlord's solicitors should be asked to advise upon.

4 To make recommendations for better handling of future cases, if appropriate.

5   To provide long-term advice and guidance to district housing managers in particularly difficult cases.

6   To make recommendations to the director of housing for policy reviews in the light of experience in individual cases.

7   To make recommendations to the director of housing and the director of the legal department, or the landlord's solicitors, on any improvements in procedures in the light of experience.

8   To identify any training needs necessary in the legal and housing departments.

9   To review any developments in council-wide strategies for dealing with racial harassment cases.

10 To monitor the effectiveness of various strategies adopted for reducing racial harassment, including the effectiveness of court actions against perpetrators, and to make any appropriate recommendations.

11 For the avoidance of doubt it is not the remit of the working party:
   (a) to make any decisions about policy
   (b) to make any decisions about procedural changes
   (c) to make any decisions on individual cases
   (d) to carry out any management of the decision-makers
   (e) to carry out any management of those responsible for implementing decisions
   (f) to implement any decision

(g) to act as a channel of information between the legal and housing departments about individual cases. Such information should pass directly, independently of the working party meetings.

BIBLIOGRAPHY

Accounting for Equality, Commission for Racial Equality, 1991

Action on Racial Harassment: legal remedies and local authorities, Duncan Forbes, Legal Action Group, 1988

Are You Doing Enough, National Federation of Housing Associations, 1992

Code of Practice in Rented Housing, the Commission for Racial Equality, 1991

Discrimination in Housing, Christopher Handy, Sweet & Maxwell, 1993

Harassment in London, London Research Centre, 1993

Housing Associations and Racial Equality, the Commission for Racial Equality, 1993

Housing Associations and Racial Equality in Scotland, Housing Equality Action Unit, 1993

Housing Black and Minority Ethnic Elders, the Federation of Black Housing Organisations, 1993

Interviewing Perpetrators of Racial Harassment, Gerard Lemos, Lemos Associates, 1993

Living in Terror: A Report on Racial Violence and Harassment in Housing, Commission for Racial Equality, 1987

London Housing Statistics 1991, London Research Centre, 1992

Making the Law Work on Racial Harassment, Duncan Forbes and Lee Bridges, Legal Action Group, 1991

Racial Attacks, The Home Office, 1981

Racial Attacks and Harassment, Third Report of the Home Affairs Committee, HMSO, 1986

Racial Harassment, the Association of Metropolitan Authorities, 1987

Racial Harassment on Local Authority Housing Estates, Commission for Racial Equality, 1981

Racial Harassment: Policies and Procedures for Housing Associations, National Federation of Housing Associations, 1989

Racial Violence and Harassment, The Runnymede Trust, 1986

The Response to Racial Attacks and Harassment, The First Report of the Inter-Departmental Racial Attacks Group, Home Office, 1989

The Response to Racial Attacks: Sustaining the Momentum, Second Report of the Inter-Departmental Racial Attacks Group, The Home Office, 1991

Room For All: Tenants Associations and Race Equality, the Commission for Racial Equality, 1993

Training for Racial Equality: A guide, Commission for Racial Equality, 1989

ACKNOWLEDGEMENTS

The authors gratefully acknowledge permission to reproduce on pages 50 and 51 an extract from Duncan Forbes and Lee Bridges' *Making the Law Work on Racial Harassment*, Legal Action Group, 1991.

OTHER TITLES IN THE SERIES

Eliminating Racial Harassment is one of a series of guides for housing managers.

Interviewing Perpetrators of Racial Harassment

Published in 1993, this guide describes the common reactions of perpetrators of racial harassment, and gives detailed guidance of how to conduct interviews to stop racial harassment.

Supporting Those Experiencing Racial Harassment

Due to be published in 1994, this book will advise on how to give practical and emotional support to those experiencing racial harassment, so that they feel less vulnerable and are able to participate in stopping the harassment, with the support of the landlord.

Legal Remedies for Dealing with Racial Harassment

Currently in preparation, this book will give practical guidance for housing managers on what legal provisions, such as possession, injunctions and criminal proceedings, can be used in cases of racial harassment, and how to go about using these remedies.

Case Studies on Dealing with Racial Harassment

A review of previous cases of racial harassment, how they were handled by local authorities and housing associations, and what the outcomes were.